IF GEORGE ORWELL WERE ALIVE TODAY . . . ON *NINETEEN EIGHTY-FOUR* AND THE THRUST OF ORWELLIAN SATIRE

IF GEORGE ORWELL WERE ALIVE TODAY . . . ON *NINETEEN EIGHTY-FOUR* AND THE THRUST OF ORWELLIAN SATIRE

JOHN DALE

PAMPHLETEER

Pamphleteer is an Australian Scholarly imprint.

First published 2019 by
Australian Scholarly Publishing Pty Ltd
7 Lt Lothian St Nth, North Melbourne, Vic 3051
Tel: 03 9329 6963 / Fax: 03 9329 5452
enquiry@scholarly.info / www.scholarly.info

ISBN 978-1-925801-87-3

Cover design: Wayne Saunders

Contents

Introduction

If George Orwell were alive today what would his politics be? The conservative intellectual Norman Podhoretz posed this question back in 1983 for a cover story in *Harper's* magazine, and concluded, rather unconvincingly, that Orwell would have sided with the neo-conservatives and against the left. For Podhoretz, Orwell's driving passion was his opposition to totalitarianism.

In Nazi Germany and the Soviet Union, totalitarianism had established itself to such a degree that every aspect of human life was subjected to state control, and with the defeat of the Nazi regime in May 1945, it was the communist version of totalitarianism that inspired Orwell's two great political satires *Animal Farm* and *Nineteen Eighty-Four*.

If Orwell had lived through the height of the Cold War, Podhoretz argued, he would have come to identify with the neo-cons in Washington under Ronald Reagan, many of them Jewish intellectuals who had started on the left but became strongly opposed to Soviet expansionism. 'More than anything else, the ethos of the left-wing literary intelligentsia was Orwell's true subject and the one that elicited his most brilliant work' (Podhoretz, 1983: 50).

It is interesting, though futile, to speculate how a writer may have changed their political views had they lived. Particularly when we have Orwell's own words to prove that up until his death in January 1950 he remained a democratic socialist:

> Every line of serious work that I have written since 1936 has been written, directly or indirectly *against* totalitarianism and *for* democratic Socialism, as I understand it. (Orwell, 2003 [1946]: 7)

Orwell's concept of a democratic socialist was one with an emphasis on democracy and liberty in contrast to the Soviet interpretation of socialism with its collectivisation of farm lands, dictatorship of the proletariat and repressive state apparatus. The major difference between democratic socialism and Soviet-style communism was the means to the end.

> In the name of Socialism the Russian regime has committed almost every crime that can be imagined, but at the same time its evolution was *away* from Socialism, unless one redefines the word in terms that no Socialist of 1917 would have accepted … The formula usually employed is 'You can't make an omelette without breaking eggs'. And if one replies, 'Yes, but where is the omelette?', the answer is likely to be: 'Oh well, you can't expect everything to happen all in a moment'. (Orwell and Angus, 2000d: 16)

Orwell and totalitarianism

What is unique about Orwell and one of the reasons he continues to be so widely admired is that unlike many of his fellow writers on the left – Auden, Spender, Day-Lewis – he spoke truthfully about what was occurring in the Soviet Union, the millions dying in the Gulag. In 1941, Orwell wrote to the Dickens scholar Humphry House: 'All people who are morally sound, have known since about 1931 that the Russian regime stinks' (Orwell and Angus, 2000a: 532). And in 1945, he wrote to the Duchess of Athol: 'I belong to the Left and must work inside it, much as I hate Russian totalitarianism and its poisonous influence in this country' (Orwell and Angus, 2000d: 30). In a BBC radio broadcast in May

1941, Orwell expressed his fears of totalitarianism expanding world-wide:

> Totalitarianism has abolished freedom of thought to an extent unheard of in any previous age. And it is important to realise that its control of thought is not only negative, but positive. It not only forbids you to express – even to *think* – certain thoughts, but it dictates what you *shall* think, it creates an ideology for you, it tries to govern your emotional life as well as setting up a code of conduct … the totalitarian state tries to control the thoughts and emotions of its subjects at least as completely as it controls their actions. (Orwell and Angus, 2000b: 135)

It was this control of the political combined with the personal that troubled Orwell most. In the history of despotism and tyranny, he saw totalitarianism as a new and higher stage: a system of government centralised and dictatorial which demands the complete subservience of the individual to the state. Orwell's biographer Bernard Crick also believed Orwell had come to fear totalitarian governments as the greater menace to humanity:

> If totalitarianism becomes our common way of life, then all other humane values, liberty, fraternity, social justice, love of literature, love of plain speaking and clear writing, belief in a natural moral decency among ordinary people, love of nature, enjoyment of human oddity, and patriotism would perish. (Crick, 1981: 398–9)

What is so important about Orwell and why, in the words of Christopher Hitchens (2002), Orwell still matters, is that his allegiance was to the truth. Free speech, liberty, freedom of thought and the exchange of ideas were the values he supported.

> The really frightening thing about totalitarianism is not that it commits 'atrocities' but that it attacks the concept of objective truth: it claims to control the past as well as the future. (Orwell and Angus, 2000c: 88)

Both left and right continue today to claim Orwell as one of their own, but there can be no doubt that he remained a genuine socialist up until his death and detested the authoritarian nature of totalitarian regimes.

A far more intriguing question than the one Podhoretz posed – and one that I wish to explore in this paper – is what *Nineteen Eighty-Four* would be like if it were written today?

A near future

Seventy years after its publication on 8 June 1949, *Nineteen Eighty-Four* remains very much a product of post-war England – with its food shortages and 'bombed sites where the plaster dust swirled in the air and the willow-herb straggled over the heaps of rubble' (Orwell, 1984 [1949]: 5) – rather than as a reliable predictor of a future world. But there are many things that Orwell did get right: the erosion of freedom of speech, the denial of privacy, the policing of language by governments to control thought and speech and the growing surveillance of their citizens.

Like many socialists, Orwell believed capitalism would eventually collapse and he failed to foresee that giant corporations such as Facebook and Google would become more powerful than national governments and could track everything we purchased, censor our posts and harvest our personal data.

Orwell saw a dreary socialism pervading everything apart from the proles who went about their drinking and consumption of pornography, but the hope for the future lay in their awakening. Like many writers of the period, Orwell admired the working class: 'If there was hope it lay in the proles. You had to cling on to that. When you put it in words it sounded reasonable: it was when you looked at the human beings passing you on the pavement that it became an act of faith' (Orwell, 1984 [1949]: 89).

And yet *Nineteen Eighty-Four* was never intended as a prediction so much as a warning. It is surely one of the most important novels published in the 20th century, not only because of its sales – approximately 30 million copies to date (*Hollywood Reporter*, 2017) – but also because of its influence on the English language. Like Shakespeare, Orwell has left his mark. Very few writers become eponymous adjectives and the word Orwellian has come to mean *a frightening view of a dystopian future.* Big Brother, Room 101, the Ministry of Truth and other neologisms have entered popular discourse.

Nineteen Eighty-Four is not simply a prophecy but a satire of what could happen. According to Crick, the crime writer Julian Symons called it 'a near future' (Crick, 1981: 393). At the same time *Nineteen Eighty-Four* is very much a product of a geopolitical period when the Soviet Union, the American empire and the rise of Communist China threatened to divide the world into three great spheres. In a letter to the United Automobile Workers, Orwell wrote of his intentions:

> My recent novel is NOT intended as an attack on socialism or on the British Labour Party (of which I am a supporter) but as a show-up of the perversions to which a centralized economy is liable and which have already been partly realized in Communism and Fascism. I do not believe that the kind of society

I describe necessarily *will* arrive, but I believe (allowing of course for the fact that the book is a satire) that something resembling it *could* arrive. I believe also that totalitarian ideas have root in the minds of intellectuals everywhere, and I have tried to draw these ideas out to their logical consequences .... And that totalitarianism, *if not fought against*, could triumph anywhere. (Orwell and Angus, 2000d: 502)

A changing Britain

The England Orwell depicted in the late nineteen forties was about to change dramatically, though not in the way Orwell imagined. The nineteen fifties ushered in the first waves of immigration from the Indian subcontinent including Hindus, Sikhs, and Muslims from the west part of Pakistan and from east Pakistan which became Bangladesh in 1971. From the early fifties to the late seventies England underwent a massive amount of social and cultural change, with large-scale immigration making the population ethnically far more diverse.

Race is rarely addressed in *Nineteen Eighty-Four* other than a passing description of a poster depicting the 'monstrous figure of a Eurasian soldier, three or four metres high, striding forward with expressionless

Mongolian face and enormous boots, a submachine gun pointed from his hip' (Orwell, 1984 [1949]: 183). The proles and Party members are homogenously Anglo-Saxon.

Orwell failed to foresee that religious belief would prove such a strong force in the future – an oversight recognised by Evelyn Waugh, who lived near Orwell's sanatorium and who visited him in 1949 at the behest of Malcolm Muggeridge (Crick, 1981: 387). 'What makes your version of the future spurious to me is the disappearance of the church,' Waugh wrote to him in 1948 after reading *Nineteen Eighty-Four.* 'Disregard all the supernatural implications if you like, but you must admit its unique character as a social and historical institution. I believe it is inextinguishable' (*Daily Mail,* 13 June 2009). Although the Anglican Church has since lost much of its cultural prominence, another faith is taking its place as an inextinguishable force in contemporary Britain with the projected Muslim population expected to increase from 4.6% of the UK population in 2010 to 8.2% by 2030 (Pew Research Centre, 2011).

Reactions from left and right

Orwell was someone who saw beyond the orthodoxies of his age.

> The whole argument that one mustn't speak plainly because it 'plays into the hands of' this or that sinister influence is dishonest, in the sense that people only use it when it suits them … beneath this argument there always lies the intention to do propaganda for some sectional interest, and to browbeat critics into silence by telling them they are 'objectively' reactionary. (Orwell and Angus, 2000d: 36)

Orwell continues to be claimed by both left and right. 'In the view of many on the official Left,' Hitchens wrote, 'he committed the ultimate sin of giving ammunition to the enemy. Not only did he do this in the 30s … but he repeated the offence in the opening years of the Cold War and thus – objectively, as people used to say – became an ally of the forces of conservatism' (Hitchens, 2002: 58–9).

On the right of politics, he was admired as one of the first leading intellectuals in the West to notice the stench at the heart of the Soviet Union. Orwell had experienced the influence of communism in Spain first-hand and wrote about the Soviet Revolution that all the seeds of evil were there from the start. 'And that things would not have been any different if Lenin or Trotsky had remained in control' (Orwell and Angus, 2000d: 5).

Although Orwell satirised the totalitarian nature of Stalinism and Soviet communism in *Animal Farm*, there is no doubt that he remained a democratic socialist up until his death. 'He was conservative about many things,' Hitchens (2002:

102) observed, 'but not his politics'.

Nineteen Eighty-Four is not the greatest English novel ever written – his biographer called it 'a flawed masterpiece both of literature and of political thought' (Crick, 1981: 399). But it is certainly one of the greatest fictional depictions of totalitarianism ever published. A novel of ideas rather than one of character and a masterpiece of political speculation. V.S. Pritchett declared it to be as fine as anything that Swift had ever written, a savage satire on the 'moral corruption of absolute power' (Crick, 1981: 39).

Orwell drew heavily on the writings of the American Trotskyist turned conservative, James Burnham, author of *The Managerial Revolution and The Machiavellians* (1941). His 1946 summary of Burnham's theories reads like an outline for *Nineteen Eighty-Four*:

> All historical changes finally boil down to the replacement of one ruling class by another. All talk about democracy, liberty, equality, fraternity,

all revolutionary movements, all visions of Utopia, or 'the classless society', or 'the Kingdom of Heaven on earth', are humbug (not necessarily conscious humbug) covering the ambitions of some new class which is elbowing its way to power. ... The new 'managerial' societies will not consist of a patchwork of small, independent states, but of great super-states grouped round the main industrial centres in Europe, Asia and America. These super-states will fight among themselves for possession of the remaining uncaptured portions of the earth, but will be unable to conquer one another completely. (Orwell and Angus, 2000d: 160–1)

Political orthodoxy

Orwell never used the term politically correct; but he did use the phrase politically orthodox. 'To be corrupted by totalitarianism one does not have to live in a totalitarian country. The mere presence of certain ideas can spread a kind of poison that makes one subject after another impossible for literary purposes. Wherever there is an enforced orthodoxy – or even two orthodoxies, as often happens – good writing stops' (Orwell, 2003 [1946]: 218).

It was Orwell's belief in fairness and equality while refusing to be blinded by the political orthodoxy of his age that set him apart from many of his fellow writers from the 1930s and 1940s. He condemned the hypocrisy of those on the left who supported Stalin, writers such as the French intellectual Jean-

Paul Sartre whom he described to his publisher Fred Warburg, as 'a bag of wind' (Crick, 1981: 380).

With the defeat of Nazism, Orwell saw communism as the greater threat. And with the failure of communism as a social experiment that caused a hundred million deaths, Orwell would have sensed the real danger coming from the third great totalitarian ideology of our age.

It is my contention that if Orwell were writing *Nineteen Eighty-Four* today, seventy years later, and set in a London of the near future, it would be the threat of religious fundamentalism that he would warn against. Islamist theology as practised in countries such as Saudi Arabia, Sudan, Yemen and Iran is by its very definition a totalitarian construct: a politico-religious system of absolute power where the state has no limit to its authority and regulates every aspect of public and private life. It is this emphasis on the regulation of a citizen's private life that distinguishes a totalitarian regime from a purely authoritarian regime such as Putin's Russia or Xi Jinping's China where social and economic institutions exist that are not under the government's control. Islamism is not simply a religion, but a complete cultural and political system. Sharia is far more than a set of laws. It includes theology, law, philosophy, morality, and contains instructions for the minutest details of individual behaviour, as well as regulations on the structuring of government and relations between states. It is all encompassing and has a position for every aspect of human life (BBC, 3 September 2009).

Apostasy and blasphemy may seem to us in 2019 like vestiges of medieval history, but in the Middle East and North Africa '18 of the region's 20 countries (90%) criminalise blasphemy and 14 (70%) criminalise apostasy' (Pew Research Centre, 2016). In December 2015, authorities in Sudan charged 25 men for apostasy. The men face the death penalty (Pew Research Centre, 2016). In 2018, an ethnic Chinese woman was jailed for eighteen months under Indonesia's blasphemy laws for complaining that the call to prayer was too loud from a local mosque (*Guardian*, 23 August 2018). And, in Pakistan blasphemy – defined as speech or actions considered to be contemptuous of God or the divine – is a capital crime (Pew Research Centre, 2016). A Christian mother in Pakistan, Asia Bibi, was on death row for blasphemy from 2010 until her acquittal in 2018. About a quarter of the world's countries have anti-blasphemy laws or policies, a Pew Research Centre analysis found, and more than one-in-ten nations have laws penalizing apostasy, Pakistan was one of 12 of 50 countries in the Asia-Pacific region that had strict blasphemy laws in 2014 and, during that year, blasphemy laws were enforced in several of those 12 nations (Pew Research Centre, 2016).

The United States Commission on International Religious Freedom (USCIRF), identified 71 countries that punished blasphemy. The six countries deemed to practise the grossest violations of international standards were all Muslim-majority lands: Iran, Pakistan, Yemen, Somalia, Qatar and Egypt (*Economist*, 13 August 2017).

The third totalitarian ideology

Religious fundamentalism poses a far greater danger to democracy in Europe today than fascism or communism which have both been largely discredited. There are no Fascist governments anywhere in power and only five Communist nations: Vietnam, North Korea, Laos, Cuba and China. Of these, only China, having abandoned the tenets of classical Marxism, including collective ownership of the means of production, and implementing its unique brand of state-run capitalism, has succeeded economically. The main totalitarian threat today comes not from Russia nor China, but from the spread of religious fundamentalism.

As Paul Marshall has written,

> Twenty years ago, few in the west were concerned with matters of blasphemy, apostasy or insults towards Islam. But the 21st century has seen eruptions of violence worldwide in reaction to, for example, Theo van Gogh's film *Submission*, the Danish and Swedish cartoons, Pope Benedict's XVI's Regensburg speech, Geert Wilders' film *Fitna*, and the false *Newsweek* story on Qur'an desecration. (Marshall, 2011: 57)

A campaign in 2007 by the 57 members of the Organisation of Islamic Conference (OIC) to ban criticism of Islam or Islamic governments through a UN defamation of Religious Resolution was a brazen attempt by the OIC to extend Islamic blasphemy restrictions to United Nation member states. As Marshall concludes,

> Many OIC countries have limits on speech regarding Islam that control not only ridicule and mocking language, but also what can be expressed, analysed, and argued in the political, cultural, social, economic and religious realms; in fact these limits are major means of social and political control. They coerce religious conformity and forcibly silence criticism of dominant religious ideas, especially when those dominant ideas support, and are supported by, political power. (Marshall, 2011: 57)

In 1989, Iran's Supreme Leader Grand Ayatollah Khomeini issued a decree for all 'zealous Muslims' to execute the British author Salman Rushdie for daring to 'insult Islamic sanctity' (Marshall, 2011: 57). The effect of that decree was experienced worldwide with the assassination of the Japanese translator of Rushdie's *The Satanic Verses*, the stabbing of its Italian translator, the shooting of its Norwegian publisher, the burning to death of 35 guests at a Turkish hotel hosting its Turkish publisher, and the need for Rushdie to remain under 24-hour police protection whenever he resides in Britain (Marshall, 2011: 59).

The long-term consequence of Khomeini's decree, Marshall argues, was that it,

> Heralded a worldwide movement to curb freedoms of religions and speech by attempting to export and internationalize the blasphemy rules that were already suppressing minorities and Muslim dissenters in many Muslim-majority countries. One of the major arenas in this effort has been the United Nations. (Marshall, 2011: 59)

It takes a brave writer to speak out and stand up against the prevailing orthodoxies, to withstand the threats and recriminations, and potential boycotts of their work. The American author Lionel Shriver has stated that fiction is about freedom and there should be no rules on how it should be written and that every author in the world should be able to write whatever story and character she pleases (*Straits Times*, 2016).

At the 2016 Brisbane Writers' Festival, Shriver warned of the dangers of political orthodoxy, 'Taken to their logical conclusion, ideologies recently come into vogue challenge our right to write fiction at all. Meanwhile the kind of fiction we are "allowed" to write is becoming so hedged, so circumscribed, so tippy-toe, that we'd indeed be better off not writing the anodyne drivel to begin with.' (*Guardian*, 2016).

'Good novels are not written by orthodoxy-sniffers,' Orwell wrote, 'nor by people who are conscience-stricken by their own unorthodoxy. Good novels are written by people who are *not frightened*' (Orwell, 1962 [1940]: 40).

The example of Salman Rushdie is a salutary lesson for all fiction writers in the West to be extremely wary of the kinds of characters they invent and the religious figures they explore. 'If we do choose to import representatives of protected groups,' Shriver said, 'special rules apply' (Shriver, 2016).

Many writers continue to believe there should be limits to freedoms of speech, but Shriver is not one of them. 'I sometimes think I'm one of the last hold-outs on the planet who believes in freedom of speech,' she said. 'And don't start with that but-there-have-to-be-limits business. I wouldn't even restrict "hate speech". People who speak hatefully hang themselves. They make themselves sound ugly. Let them. About the only limit I would put on free speech is incitement to violence' (*Straits Times*, 2016).

In his essay 'The Prevention of Literature', Orwell warned 'that the conscious enemies of liberty are those to whom liberty ought to mean most … To exercise your free speech you have to fight against economic pressure and against strong sections of public opinion' (Orwell, 2003 [1946]: 223).

Writers of every political persuasion try to use Orwell to buttress their views and I am no different here, but what I do admire about Orwell was how refreshingly truthful his writing was and how he spoke out against the prevailing orthodoxies of his time:

> The atmosphere of orthodoxy is always damaging to prose and above all it is completely ruinous to the novel, the most anarchical of all forms of literature. Literature as we know it is an individual thing, demanding mental honesty and a minimum of censorship. (Orwell, 1962 [1940]: 39)

The strongest taboo

Orwell was that rare writer, someone who thought for himself, someone who did not shirk from writing the truth despite the personal cost to his own work: in 1944 *Animal Farm* was initially rejected* by a dozen US publishers as well as T. S. Eliot at Faber & Faber because of its 'generally Trotskyist' and anti-Russian message (Crick, 1981: 315).

> To write in plain, vigorous language one has to think fearlessly, and if one thinks fearlessly one cannot be politically orthodox. (Orwell, 2003 [1946]: 217)

---

* Despite its great success, Orwell's earnings from *Animal Farm* by the time of his death amounted to around 12,000 pounds (Davison, 2001:229).

In his war-time diaries Orwell wrote, 'All propaganda is lies even when one is telling the truth' (Orwell and Angus, 2000b: 411). Hired by the BBC, Orwell attended that organisation's induction course and understood exactly how propaganda worked. His work at the BBC was influential in his conception of *Nineteen Eighty-Four* and he came to realise, 'how politically ignorant the majority of people are, how uninterested in anything outside their immediate affairs' (Orwell and Angus, 2000b: 413). He supported the war against Nazism which he saw as 'a war in favour of freedom of thought' and 'freedom of expression' (Orwell and Angus, 2000c: 199).

Writing about the future is fraught with failure and the most any writer can do is to warn readers about what *could* happen. If Orwell were writing *Nineteen Eighty-Four* today and set in a London of the near future it would be instantly recognisable to us as the London of our own time, where the strongest taboos for any writer in the West concern the cultural and social pressures caused by large-scale immigration and, in particular, the spread of radical Islam.

> Even a single taboo can have an all-round crippling effect upon the mind because there is always the danger that any thought which is freely followed up may lead to the forbidden thought. It follows that the atmosphere of totalitarianism is deadly to any kind of prose writer. (Orwell, 2003 [1946]: 216)

In his book *Why Orwell Matters*, Christopher Hitchens called Orwell, 'the outstanding English example of the dissident intellectual who preferred above all other allegiances the loyalty to truth' (Hitchens, 2002: 52).

What is so frightening about *Nineteen Eighty-Four* is how the state monitors your speech and controls your thoughts. It is this control over the personal that is most disturbing. And of course, the control is always justified by those who impose it under one pretext or another.

> From the totalitarian point of view history is something to be created rather than learned. A *totalitarian state is in effect a theocracy* and its ruling caste, in order to keep its position, has to be thought of as infallible. But since, in practice, no-one is infallible, it is frequently necessary to rearrange past events in order to show that this or that mistake was not made, or that this or that imaginary triumph actually happened. (Orwell, 2003 [1946]: 213, my emphasis)

The strongest taboo for any writer in the West today is no longer sexually explicit or violent material, but criticism of Islamist extremism and beliefs. 'The term *Islamophobic*, Hitchens observed, 'is already being introduced into the culture, as if it's an accusation of race hatred for example or bigotry, whereas it's only the objection to the preachings of a very extreme and absolutist religion' (Hitchens, 2012: 3.32).

As in Orwell's day, 'If you possess information that conflicts with the prevailing orthodoxy you are expected to distort it or to keep quiet about it' (Orwell, 2003 [1946]: 215).

Orwell understood how language is used to stifle debate and that for writers 'to accept political responsibility now means yielding oneself over to orthodoxies and "party lines", with all the timidity and dishonesty that that implies' (Davison, 2001: 483).

'Take away freedom of speech,' Orwell wrote in 1944, 'and the creative faculties dry up' (Orwell and Angus, 1968c: 133).

Orwell and language

The manipulation of language by governments is always intended to serve political agendas, to re-shape language in the cause of a dominant ideology. The most effective way to suppress free speech in society is to rename it. The writer Brendan O'Neill argues that it is unacceptable to repress the expression of ideas. 'We should bristle and balk as much at the idea of hate speech as we do at the idea of thoughtcrime' (*Spiked*, 10 June 2016).

> Where religion and power are entwined, states invariably draw on laws restricting speech critical of religion for other than purely religious purposes. Many OIC members silence

> their domestic opponents and critics through a wide variety of repressive measures, but one prominent tactic, especially predominant in Iran, is to accuse such critics of 'insulting Islam' or the 'Islamic regime.' These accusations enable both the crushing of political dissent and the silencing of Muslims who question the official and dominant versions of Islam – including those who advocate versions of Islam that promote human freedom. (Marshall, 2011: 63)

Orwell was not infected by the dominant Marxist ideology of his age, as much as driven by a desire to speak the truth. 'The friends of totalitarianism in this country,' he wrote, 'usually tend to argue that since absolute truth is not attainable, a big lie is no worse than a little lie' (Orwell, 2003 [1946]: 214).

He identified with the working class or common people and was suspicious of intellectuals and bureaucrats who corrupted the language for their own political purposes. He saw clearly that the rise of totalitarianism was democracy's main enemy and believed that literature was doomed if liberty of thought perished (Orwell, 2003 [1946]: 223).

Conclusion

Like many English writers of the period, Orwell placed more importance on class than culture. He did not predict the tremendous cultural shift caused by large-scale immigration from non-democratic countries which has led to a decline in support for those democratic values that he held dearly: freedom of speech, liberty and the rights of the individual.

In a 615-page survey for the 2016 Channel 4 documentary *What British Muslims Really Think* researchers found that more than 100,000 British Muslims sympathise with suicide bombers and people who commit other terrorist attacks. In addition, 23% of British Muslims said 'Islamic Sharia should replace British law in areas with large Muslim populations' (Kern, 2016).

Orwell was a brilliant essayist who recognised that writers need to blast their way through the dead hand of political orthodoxy and he would have been opposed to any ideology that strives to regulate aspects of your private life. In an editorial to *Polemic*, he wrote, 'So we arrive at the old, true, and unpalatable conclusion that a Communist and a fascist are somewhat nearer to one another than either is to a democrat' (Orwell and Angus, 2000d: 160).

If Orwell were alive today, I believe that he would warn – amongst other things – about the threat we face from the rise of the third great totalitarian ideology. Relatively few writers today are willing to write about the spread of religious fundamentalism. It is the single greatest taboo for any writer. There is little possibility of communism gaining power in Europe but there is a demographic certainty that Islamist parties such as Sweden's Jasin party or the Islam Party in Belgium will continue to grow in popularity and in influence. According to the Gatestone Institute, 'Islamist parties have already begun to emerge in many European countries, such as the Netherlands, Austria, Belgium and France' (Bergman, 2017).

In the UK the government's Commissioner for Countering Extremism, Sara Khan, has warned that hard-line Islamist groups are 'weaponising Islamophobia and cynically using human rights to promote their ideology' (*Telegraph*, 2018).

Nineteen Eighty-Four speaks to our time just as strongly as it did when it was published seventy years ago. There are many reasons why Orwell has survived and why he continues to be so relevant, and they include the strength of his prose and the courage of his views. Perhaps there has been no more critical period since the 1930s when our basic freedoms of expression have been under threat. In the unused preface to *Animal Farm* Orwell wrote, 'If liberty means anything at all it means the right to tell people what they do not want to hear' (Crick, 1981: 319).

Orwell was a truly significant writer who recognised that without intellectual liberty, creativity withers away (Orwell, 1962 [1940]: 39).

If Orwell were writing *Nineteen Eighty-Four* today, he would warn that the dangers to democracy now come from a new direction and the writers of our time must do what Orwell did: face up to the truth and write fearlessly.

References

Bergman, J (2017) 'Europe: What do Islamic Parties Want', *Gatestone Institute*, 29 September. Available online at https://www.gatestoneinstitute.org/11017/europe-islamic-parties, accessed on 10 September 2018

Crick, Bernard (1981) *George Orwell: A Life,* London: Secker & Warburg

Davison, Peter (ed.) (2001) *George Orwell: Orwell and Politics,* London: Penguin

Guardian (2016) 'I hope the concept of cultural appropriation is a passing fad', Tuesday, 13 September

Hitchens, Christopher (2002) *Why Orwell Matters*, New York: Basic Books

Hitchens, Christopher (2009) 'Islamophobia and Freedom of Speech'. Available online at https://www.youtube.com/watch?v=0EYg8Tgrh0o, accessed on 10 September 2018

Hollywood Reporter (2017), 'Summer Broadway Opening Set for 1984'. Available online at https://www.

hollywoodreporter.com/news/summer-broadway-opening-set-1984-971662, accessed on 11 September 2018

Kern, S (2016) 'What British Muslims Really Think', *Gatestone Institute*, 17 April. Available online at https://www.gatestoneinstitute.org/7861/british-muslims-survey, accessed on 10 September 2018

Lewis, Peter (1981) *George Orwell: The Road to 1984*, London: Heinemann

Marshall, Paul (2011) 'Exporting blasphemy restrictions: the organisation of the Islamic conference and the United Nations', *The Review of Faith & International Affairs*, Vol. 9, No. 2, pp. 57–63

O'Neill, Brendan (2016) 'We must have the freedom to hate', *Spiked*, 10 June. Available online at https://www.spiked-online.com/2016/06/10/we-must-have-the-freedom-to-hate-2/, accessed on 9 September 2018

Orwell, George (1962) [1940] *Inside the Whale and other essays,* London: Penguin

Orwell, George (1984) [1949] *Nineteen Eighty-Four,* Penguin: Middlesex

Orwell, George (2003) [1946] *Shooting an Elephant and Other Essays*, Penguin: London

Orwell, Sonia, and Angus, Ian (eds.) (1968) *The Collected Essays, Journalism and Letters of George Orwell; Volume 1: An Age Like This, 1920–1940*. Secker and Warburg: London

Orwell, Sonia, and Angus, Ian(eds.) (1968) *The Collected Essays, Journalism and Letters of George Orwell; Volume 2: My Country Right or Left, 1940–1943,* Secker and Warburg: London

Orwell, Sonia, and Angus, Ian (eds.) (1968) *The Collected Essays, Journalism and Letters of George Orwell; Volume 3: As I Please, 1943–1945*, Secker and Warburg: London

Orwell, Sonia, and Angus, Ian (eds.) (1968) *The Collected Essays, Journalism and Letters of George Orwell; Volume 4: In Front of Your Nose, 1945–1950*, Secker and Warburg: London

Pew Research Centre (2011), *Muslim Population by Country*, accessed on 10 September 2018, http://www.pewforum.org/2011/01/27/table-muslim-population-by-country

Pew Research Centre (2016), *Which countries still outlaw apostasy and blasphemy,* 29 July, accessed on 10 September 2018, http://www.pewresearch.org/fact-tank/2016/07/29/which-countries-still-outlaw-apostasy-and-blasphemy

Podhoretz, Norman (1983) 'If Orwell Were Alive Today', *Quadrant,* Vol. 27, No. 10, pp. 48–53

Straits Times (2016) 'American author Lionel Shriver is a champion of free speech', 1 November

Telegraph (2018) 'Hardline groups are "weaponizing" Islamophobia', 16 September

About the Author

John Dale is a Professor of Writing at UTS. He is the author of seven books including the best-selling *Huckstepp* and three crime novels. His campus novel, *Leaving Suzie Pye*, was translated into Turkish and he has written a novella *Plenty*. He has published a memoir, *Wild Life*, and edited three anthologies, including the recent *Sydney Noir* (2019). His essays, reviews and non-fiction have appeared in a variety of journals and newspapers; his research and teaching areas include narrative fiction, creative non-fiction and crime narratives. This article appeared online in the international journal *New Writing*.

Printed in Australia
AUHW020844120221
341141AU00011B/45

9 781925 801873